GREAT BRITONS

SCIENTISTS

Jenny Vaughan

FRANKLIN WATTS
LONDON•SYDNEY

First published in 2007 by
Franklin Watts

Copyright © Franklin Watts
2007

Franklin Watts
338 Euston Road
London NW1 3BH

Franklin Watts Australia
Level 17/207 Kent Street
Sydney, NSW 2000

A CIP catalogue record for
this book is available from
the British Library.

Dewey number: 509.0092

ISBN: 978 0 7496 7469 4

Printed in China

Franklin Watts is a division of
Hachette Children's Books, an
Hachette Livre UK company.

Designer: Thomas Keenes
Art Director: Jonathan Hair
Editor: Sarah Ridley
Editor-in-Chief:
John C. Miles
Picture Research:
Diana Morris

Picture credits:
Alinari/Topfoto: 31.
British Library/HIP/Topfoto:
25. Mary Evans Picture
Library: 15, 27. Fortean
Picture Library/Topfoto: 7.
Fotomas/Topfoto: 10, 13, 23.
John Hedgecoe/Topfoto: 39.
PA/Topham: 32, 43.
Picturepoint/Topham: 9, 28,
37. Science Photo Library: 21.
Time & Life Pictures/Getty
Images: 35. Topfoto: front
cover, 17, 18, 40. UPP/Topfoto:
45.

Every attempt has been made
to clear copyright. Should
there be any inadvertent
omission please apply to the
publisher for rectification.

CONTENTS

INTRODUCTION

Science, as we know it today, is something relatively new to Britain. For the origins of mathematics, much of physics, chemistry, medicine and biology, we must go back hundreds, sometimes thousands, of years and look to the Middle East, India, Greece and Rome.

British – and European – science did not really get started until the 1600s, when superstition and magic gradually gave way to serious scholarship. This book starts at the time this changeover was beginning, with the story of John Dee. Considered a magician and conjurer even in his own lifetime, he was also a seeker after knowledge – as all scientists are.

After John Dee came a whole series of great scientists: Robert Boyle – who was born in Ireland but who lived and worked in England; Sir Isaac Newton, one of the most important scientists of all time; and the astronomers Edmond Halley and German-born Sir William Herschel and his sister Caroline. Michael Faraday, whose theories about electricity are still accepted today, worked during the 19th century, as did the great naturalist Charles Darwin, the computer pioneer Charles Babbage and the physicists William Thomson (Lord Kelvin) and James Clerk Maxwell. In the 20th century, New Zealand-born physicist Ernest

Rutherford founded nuclear physics while working in Manchester and Cambridge, and Alan Turing became the first modern computer programmer. The tradition of great British scientists continues to this day.

But science is not something that happens in isolation. Modern scientists tend to work in teams, rather than individuals – this is not really something new. Many scientists in the past have also worked in teams – sometimes working side-by-side with colleagues, or by keeping in close touch with fellow-scientists from overseas. And all have built on discoveries made by men and women from other periods of history, and from other countries, who shared their works and ideas. This is how science develops and grows.

Some of the greatest scientists of all time have been British, and many appear in this book. But these are not the only great British scientists – there have been, and will be, many more. You may well know of, or find out about others, which you can add to this list. ⚑

JOHN DEE

ELIZABETH I'S TEACHER

BORN London,
13 July 1527
DIED Mortlake, near London,
26 March 1608
AGE 80

John Dee was a magician, an alchemist and an astrologer – as well as a mathematician and a scientist who excelled in physics, astronomy and geography. He is believed to be the model for the scholar-magician, Prospero, in Shakespeare's *The Tempest*.

Dee's father, who served in the court of Henry VIII, sent his 16-year-old son to study at Cambridge University. After graduating, young John studied in Brussels with the cartographer (map-maker) Gerardus Mercator. He began to collect astronomical and mathematical instruments and became expert in navigation. Later, he prepared charts for the explorer Sebastian Cabot and taught navigation to his crews.

By 1555, he was back in England, where the new queen, Mary I, had him imprisoned for 'calculating' – possibly casting horoscopes – which she saw as a form of magic. As a devout Catholic, she disapproved of such things. Once released, Dee tried to persuade Mary to support a plan for a Royal Library, which other scholars could use. Though nothing came of this, he built up a massive library of his own. When Elizabeth I came to the throne, Dee became her astrologer and science tutor.

For Dee – as for other scholars of his time – there was no clear line between 'science' and the supernatural. All forms of study were attempts to find out about the universe. In the 1580s, when alchemy and magic dominated his life, he spent several years travelling in Europe. Returning to England in 1589, he found that much of his library had been stolen, along with his mathematical instruments. He spent the end of his working life in Manchester

Alchemy

Alchemy was an ancient science, originating in the Middle East. One of its chief goals was to discover how to turn less valuable metals into gold. It was also a serious study of the nature of substances.

where, in 1605, his wife and several of his children died of the plague. He returned to London, and died three years later.

For many years, John Dee was seen as little more than a conjurer. Recently, scientists have realised that there was more to his studies than magic.

ROBERT BOYLE
FORMULATED 'BOYLE'S LAW'

BORN Lismore Castle,
County Waterford,
Ireland,
25 January, 1627
DIED London,
20 December, 1691
AGE 64

Robert Boyle is regarded as one of the greatest-ever scientists, and was among the first to rely on experimentation as a means of proving scientific truths. In many ways, he was one of the first modern scientists.

Boyle was the youngest son of the Earl of Cork. Although born in Ireland, he can be thought of as British because, at the time, Ireland was considered to be part of Britain.

After finishing his education, Boyle went to live in Dorset in a house he had inherited from his father. There, he set up a laboratory, carried out experiments and studied living things through a microscope.

In 1655, he moved to Oxford. There, he began experimenting with the properties of air, using a vacuum chamber and air pump, which he had employed his young assistant, Robert Hooke (1635–1703), to make. This was one of the first rigorous series of experiments in scientific history. It was during these that Boyle realised that when a gas is compressed, its pressure increases proportionately. So, for example, if the pressure a gas is subject to doubles, then its volume halves, and if the pressure halves, its volume doubles. This is called 'Boyle's law'.

Boyle also experimented with chemistry, and was – like other scholars of his time – deeply interested in alchemy. He was one of the first scientists to challenge the ancient idea that all existence is made up of four elements (earth, air, fire and water). Instead he thought there was a range of elements, made up of single substances, which combined to make up compounds.

Boyle described his experiments in great detail in his many books. Recording experiments in this way, so that other scientists can try them too, is normal today, but it was rarely done at the time.

Robert Boyle lived in a great age of scientists, when modern science came into being.

SIR ISAAC NEWTON
ONE OF THE GREATEST SCIENTISTS OF ALL TIME

BORN Woolsthorpe,
Lincolnshire,
4 January 1643
DIED London,
31 March 1727
AGE 84

Sir Isaac Newton is one of the world's greatest scientists. He is still remembered for his work on light, motion and gravity, and in mathematics.

A difficult man, Isaac Newton had few friends in his lifetime. Yet his achievements were so great that he is honoured by fellow-scientists to this day.

After an isolated, country childhood, Newton went to Cambridge University in 1661, where he spent most of his working life. Here he made revolutionary advances in mathematics, optics, physics and astronomy.

It was Newton who realised that colourless 'white' light is made up of a mixture of colours. He showed that, when a beam of light is refracted (bent) by passing it through a glass prism, each colour bends at a different angle. The colours can then be seen separately, as a spectrum. Newton also developed a reflecting telescope (using mirrors rather than lenses) – the basis for many modern telescopes.

Newton formulated three laws of motion – rules about how things move. He also came to understand gravity. The story goes that, in 1665, while at his family home, he observed an apple fall, and realised that there is a force, gravity, that attracts objects to each other. He was able to calculate how gravity relates to the masses of the objects and their distance apart. He saw that gravity affects the motion of the Moon – holding it in place as it orbits the Earth.

Newton is also said to have discovered the mathematical system, calculus, although the German Gottfried Leibniz (1646-1716) claimed this, too.

In 1693, after a nervous breakdown, Newton moved to London to run the Royal Mint. In 1703, he was elected president of the Royal Society (see page 12), a post he held until he died. In 1708, Queen Anne awarded him a knighthood.

Just before his death, he said, '… I seem to have been only like a boy playing on the sea-shore … now and then finding a smoother pebble or a prettier shell than ordinary, whilst the great ocean of truth lay all undiscovered before me.'

Despite his position as a pioneer of modern science, Newton still clung to some of the more ancient scientific ideas, especially alchemy, which he believed was possible. It also appears that he invented the cat-flap!

Robert Hooke

ROBERT HOOKE (1635-1703) was Robert Boyle's assistant and an important scientist in his own right. He was a rival to Newton in the studies of gravity and light – but his work was overshadowed by Newton's, and the two men became bitter enemies. Newton did, in a letter to Hooke, admit his own debt to other scientists – which may have included Hooke: 'If I have seen a little further,' he wrote, 'it is by standing on the shoulders of giants.' However, some historians believe he was simply being unkind, as Hooke was a very short man.

EDMOND HALLEY
IDENTIFIED HALLEY'S COMET

BORN Shoreditch,
London,
8 November 1656
DIED Greenwich,
London,
14 January 1742
AGE 85

Edmond Halley is remembered today chiefly because of a famous comet that is named after him, but his interests were far wider: as well as the stars, he studied the winds and weather, statistics, tides, and much more.

Halley became expert in astronomy while he was still at school in London. When he went to Oxford as a student in 1673 he already had a fine collection of scientific instruments for observing the stars.

Midway through his time as a student, Halley travelled to the remote South Atlantic island of St Helena to map the stars of the Southern Hemisphere. Halley also used this time for other studies, including the 'transit of Mercury' (observing the planet Mercury as it crossed the face of the Sun).

On his return, Halley graduated from Oxford, became a Fellow of the Royal Society and was recognised as one of the world's leading astronomers – at still only 22. Soon afterwards, his father mysteriously died – possibly murdered – leaving Halley without any financial support.

The Royal Society

The Royal Society was founded in 1660, when, after a lecture by the architect **SIR CHRISTOPHER WREN** (1632-1723), 12 scholars decided to found 'a Colledge for the Promoting of Physico-Mathematicall Experimentall Learning'. This group included Wren himself and **ROBERT BOYLE** (see pages 8-9). The Society met weekly to discuss science and observe experiments. It also published books – which included *Micrographia* by **ROBERT HOOKE** (see page 11). From the beginning, all members were elected to the Society, but it was not until the middle of the 19th century that membership was restricted to leading scientists.

Edmond Halley. One of his greatest achievements was his support of Sir Isaac Newton.

To overcome this, Halley hoped to take up a post at Oxford University but the Astronomer Royal, John Flamsteed (1646-1719), disapproved of Halley's religious beliefs and prevented this. (Unusually for his time, Halley did not believe that the whole Bible was literally true.) However, Halley managed to earn enough through writing and editing. He even paid for Sir Isaac Newton to publish his important work on mathematics: *Principia Mathematica Philosophiae Naturalis*. Newton, a difficult man, always remained friends with Halley.

From around 1695, Halley began a special study of comets. He realised that a comet he had observed in 1682 re-appeared regularly every 76 years. This, now known as Halley's Comet, was last seen in 1986.

Halley became Astronomer Royal in 1720, and held the post until he died. 🇬🇧

13

SIR WILLIAM HERSCHEL
DISCOVERED URANUS

BORN Hanover,
Germany,
15 November 1738
DIED Slough,
25 August 1822
AGE 83

Sir William Herschel was an astronomer whose most important discovery was the distant, giant planet Uranus. Although German by birth, both he and his sister Caroline – also an astronomer – spent most of their working lives in Britain, mainly in Bath and in Berkshire.

Caroline Herschel

Herschel's sister, **CAROLINE HERSCHEL** (1750-1848), was a musician (a concert singer). After joining her brother in England in 1772, she spent many years as his assistant and went on to make a number of important observations of her own, including the discovery of eight comets. It is said that Caroline started life with a huge disadvantage as her mother did not believe that girls should be educated, though her father gave her lessons in secret. Her eventual importance as an astronomer was recognised by the Royal Society in 1825, when she was one of the first two women to be made honorary members. She was also honoured in her native Germany, where she returned to live, and where she died at the very great age of 98.

Herschel observed the Moon, calculating the heights of its mountains, and discovered a number of double stars. He was the first person to describe the shape of our own galaxy, the Milky Way, and to estimate the distance to a star. He also carried out experiments that led him to discover infra-red radiation – light outside the visible spectrum.

Herschel settled in England at the age of 19. Originally a musician, but always fascinated by the stars, he built his own reflecting telescope. Through this, in 1781, he saw what he at first thought to be a comet, but soon realised was an unknown planet. It was eventually named Uranus.

King George III appointed Herschel as King's Astronomer, with a grant that made it possible for him to move to a house near Windsor and take up

William Herschel and his sister Caroline. The Herschels made numerous discoveries about the nature of the universe.

astronomy full time. Herschel also made over 400 telescopes, one with a 12 m (40 ft) focal length. Using this, he was able to see two moons of Saturn.

Herschel was made a knight in 1816 and founded the Astronomical Society (later the Royal Astronomical Society) in 1820. His son, John (1792-1871), was an important astronomer in his own right. 🇬🇧

15

MICHAEL FARADAY
PIONEER IN ELECTRICITY

BORN Newington
Butts, London,
22 September 1791
DIED Hampton Court,
near London,
25 August 1867
AGE 75

Michael Faraday was one of the greatest of all experimental physicists. He is best remembered for his work on electricity, and for developing the idea of fields of electromagnetic force. This underpins all of modern physics.

Faraday was the son of a blacksmith, whose formal education ended when he was 13. He was apprenticed to a bookbinder and took the opportunity to read some of the books he worked on. From this, he developed an interest in science, and began to attend classes. In 1812 he heard Sir Humphrey Davy lecture at the Royal Institution (a centre for debate and public education about science). Faraday asked Davy for a job, and became his assistant. He then began to work on his own projects.

The Danish physicist Hans Oersted (1771-1851) had already found that an electric current can produce a magnetic field. In 1821 Faraday used this fact to produce the first electric motor. Around ten years later, Faraday proved that Oersted's discovery worked in reverse – just as electricity can create a magnet, so magnetism can be used to make electricity. (The American physicist Joseph Henry [1797-1878] made the same discovery at much the same time.) This was electromagnetic induction – the

Sir Humphrey Davy

It is often said that the greatest discovery of **SIR HUMPHREY DAVY** (1778-1829) was Michael Faraday. However, Davy was a highly respected scientist in his own time. He started work as a pharmacist, and went on to become a leading chemist. He discovered sodium and potassium, and learned to make nitrous oxide. A practical man, one of his most important inventions was the miner's safety lamp, used to detect poisonous gas. Davy took Faraday on a journey through Europe between 1813 and 1815, meeting many scientists of the day. He died young, probably from inhaling chemicals.

basis for the dynamo or electric generator, and the transformer, which can change the amount of electricity that passes along a wire. Faraday also found ways of measuring the strength of electricity.

In the 1830s, Faraday went on to study electrolysis – the way in which an electrical current can break compounds down into the elements from which they are made.

Faraday was the first to develop the idea of fields of force, which was crucial to the discovery of electromagnetic radiation, including light. In 1845, he managed to prove, experimentally, that light could be affected by magnetism, and that there must therefore be a connection between the two. This discovery remains vital to the study of physics to this day.

Faraday believed in the importance of educating the public about science. He organised lectures for adults and children at the Royal Institution.

CHARLES BABBAGE
COMPUTER PIONEER

BORN Walworth,
Surrey,
26 December 1791
DIED London,
20 October 1871
AGE 79

Charles Babbage was a mathematician, an economist and, above all, an inventor. But his most famous invention was something that was never built – the ancestor of the modern computer.

Babbage firmly believed that science had an important part to play in the development of industry.

In an age before calculators, people used lists of tables (already worked out calculations) as a short-cut to doing mathematical work. These were especially important, for example, to sailors and engineers. But they were often wrong, because of mistakes in calculation and printers' errors.

Babbage studied at Cambridge University until 1817, before settling in London. In 1821, he began work on his Difference Engine, which could calculate the tables accurately and automatically, and print them out. It had 25,000 parts, and only sections of it were ever completed. The biggest problem was that it was not possible, at the time, to make the parts accurately enough. In 1833, Babbage stopped work on the Difference Engine and began a new project, which he called his Analytical Engine.

The Difference Engine would only add up in a particular order. The Analytical Engine would do several different tasks, and could be programmed, using punched cards. The way it worked was much like a modern computer, but without electronic circuits. It had a 'store' where numbers and the ongoing results of calculations could be held – like the memory in a modern computer. It also had a 'mill' (like a processor), where calculation was done. Like the first Difference Engine, it was never completed. If it had been, it would have

Ada Lovelace

ADA LOVELACE (1815-1852) was the daughter of the poet Lord Byron, but never knew her father, as her parents separated when she was still a baby. She became interested in Babbage's ideas for calculating engines and foresaw how these might be used for much more than calculating – perhaps to help scientists, or to create music. She worked out plans for using the Analytical Engine, and so is sometimes called the first computer programmer. (Babbage called her his 'fairy interpreter'.) She was wealthy and beautiful – but her life was troubled. She gambled heavily, and lost thousands of pounds (she even tried, with Babbage, to work out a system for winning on horse-races). She also had problems with drink and the drug opium – probably because she was ill and in great pain. She died of cancer, aged only 37.

been enormous, and would have needed a steam engine to power it.

In 1847, Babbage went on to design Difference Engine No 2. This, too, was never completed during his lifetime, but was built by engineers at London's Science Museum, 200 years after Babbage's birth. 🇬🇧

MARY ANNING
'THE GREATEST FOSSILIST'

BORN Lyme Regis, Dorset, 21 May 1799
DIED Lyme Regis, Dorset, 9 March 1847
AGE 47

Mary Anning has been called 'the greatest fossilist the world ever knew', despite being a poor woman, who lived at a time when even wealthy women were hardly ever taken seriously as scholars. She made her first important discovery when she was only 11 years old.

Mary Anning's family lived in the Dorset seaside town of Lyme Regis. Her father was a cabinet-maker, who made a little extra money collecting fossils and selling them from the cliffs around the town. His family often helped him. He died when Mary was only 11, leaving the family penniless.

Mary and her brother continued to search for fossils to sell. While their father was alive, they were among the first people to find part of the remains of a prehistoric sea-reptile, a bit like a dolphin, which we now call an ichthyosaur. A year later, Mary found the rest of the skeleton.

Dinosaur hunters

In the early 1800s, more and more scientists were becoming interested in fossils and fossil-hunting. These included **GIDEON MANTELL** (1790-1852), a country doctor from Sussex. In 1812, his wife, **MARY**, discovered some giant fossil teeth amongst rocks left at the roadside. Mantell learned that the rocks had come from a nearby quarry – where he found much of the skeleton of a giant, plant-eating reptile. He called this iguanodon. It was the first fossil of a dinosaur ever found. The name 'dinosaur' ('terrible lizard') was thought up by **SIR RICHARD OWEN** (1804-1892), the founder of London's Natural History Museum. The name stuck, though we now know that some were quite small, and that others were not related to lizards. Owen studied all the dinosaur fossils he could find and, after some persuasion, accepted that they were the remains of creatures that no longer existed.

Mary went on to become a skilled collector and identifier of fossils, supporting her family by selling her finds. In addition to the ichthyosaur, she also discovered the first fossil plesiosaur (a strange-looking sea-reptile, with a long neck). She became respected by many of the great palaeontologists of her age. Towards the end of her life, the Geological Society of London decided to pay her an allowance. This was an amazing decision from an organisation that did not accept women members until 1904. After Mary died at the age of 47, she was all but forgotten. However, today she is properly recognised at last. 🇬🇧

Mary Anning, carrying her pick-axe, which she used to dig fossils out of the cliffs at Lyme Regis.

CHARLES DARWIN
FIRST TO EXPLAIN THE THEORY OF EVOLUTION

BORN Shrewsbury, Shropshire, 12 February 1809
DIED Down House, Downe, Kent, 19 April 1882
AGE 73

Charles Darwin was one of the greatest naturalists of all time. He was the first scientist to understand, explain and try to prove a theory of evolution through 'natural selection', that is, how new species of living things develop.

After leaving Cambridge University in 1831, Darwin joined the Royal Navy survey ship, HMS *Beagle*, as ship's naturalist. He studied the geology and wildlife of South America and the remote Galapagos Islands in the Pacific Ocean. He saw that many of the plants and animals of the Galapagos were similar to those from South America – but not quite the same. It was as if they had reached the islands, and then changed. He also noticed that every island had its own species of finch – each with a beak that was especially well adapted to the kind of food available. When Darwin returned to England, he studied the work of other scientists, and talked to farmers who bred different kinds of animals. Gradually, he formed his theory of natural selection. This happens because few living things – even if they have the same parents –

Biologists in the 19th century

Darwin was not the only person to suggest that living things can, and do, evolve over time. His grandfather, **ERASMUS DARWIN** (1731-1802), had also believed that animals change over generations, as did the French biologist **BAPTISTE CHEVALIER DE LAMARCK** (1744-1829). Darwin had also studied the work of the American **WILLIAM CHARLES WELLS** (1757-1817) and the Scottish fruit-grower **PATRICK MATTHEW** (1790-1874), both of whom had suggested the idea of natural selection. Darwin's supporters among British biologists included the science writer, **THOMAS HUXLEY** (1825-1895). His most important supporter was probably **ALFRED RUSSEL WALLACE** (1823-1913), who also developed the theory of natural selection, but with less evidence than Darwin.

Darwin suggested a shocking idea for the time – that people, apes and monkeys might share similar ancestors. This cartoon is an attack on Darwin.

are exactly alike. Some may have an extra 'something' that helps them survive. In the case of the Galapagos finches, that 'something' was a particular kind of beak. Better-adapted finches produced better-adapted young. Gradually, new species evolved. Darwin was afraid to publish his theories, as he knew they would be fiercely attacked by the Church, which taught that all species were created by God. But, in 1858, he learned that another naturalist, Alfred Russel Wallace, was developing ideas very like his own after travelling in the Far East. Darwin quickly published his own theory, first in 1858, as a paper, then in his famous book: *On the Origin of Species by Natural Selection.*

WILLIAM THOMSON, LORD KELVIN

PIONEER OF THERMODYNAMICS AND ELECTROMAGNETIC THEORY

BORN Belfast,
24 June 1824
DIED Largs, Ayrshire,
17 December 1907
AGE 83

One of the 'giants' of British science, William Thomson was a physicist and electrical engineer. He was one of the first people to become very rich from his scientific work.

Thomson began studying at Glasgow University when he was ten years old (at the time, the University ran classes for talented children). After graduating – as an adult student – he went to Cambridge where he studied mathematics, and became interested in physics, especially electricity. He later developed apparatus for measuring electricity.

Thomson studied heat, and developed the Second Law of Thermodynamics: that heat cannot pass from a cooler body to a hotter one. He also suggested a new way of measuring temperature, the Kelvin scale. The lowest point of this scale – 0°K (also called absolute zero) – is the coldest possible temperature.

One of Thomson's greatest achievements was in overseeing the laying of a cable across the Atlantic to carry telegraphic

The First Law of Thermodynamics

JAMES PRESCOTT JOULE (1818-1889) was a physicist who worked closely with Lord Kelvin. His studies led him to establish the theory of the mechanical equivalence of heat. This theory says that, as work (movement) and heat are both forms of energy, we can calculate the amount of work needed to create a given amount of heat. This led to the development of the First Law of Thermodynamics, which says that energy cannot be created or destroyed. The unit used to measure energy – either as heat or work – is named the joule. Joule also worked with Thomson on the study of gas molecules, and discovered that if gases are allowed to expand, they cool.

24

signals between Britain and the USA. In 1857, Thomson travelled aboard the ship HMS *Agamemnon*, in a first, failed, attempt. In 1866, the cable was laid, and Thomson was knighted for his achievements.

Although Kelvin was a brilliant scientist, he had 'blind spots'. A vehement opponent of Darwin (see pages 22-23), he set about using his Second Law of Thermodynamics to prove that the Earth

was only 40 million years old – not long enough to support Darwin's theory. (We now know that Kelvin's calculations were wrong.) He refused to believe in atoms or radioactivity and thought that manned flight, other than by balloon, was impossible. He also opposed allowing women to study at Cambridge University.

Thomson was given the title Baron Kelvin (Lord Kelvin) in 1892.

JAMES CLERK MAXWELL
PIONEERING PHYSICIST

BORN Edinburgh,
13 June 1831
DIED Cambridge,
5 November 1879
AGE 48

James Clerk Maxwell is best remembered for his theories about electromagnetic fields and waves. This led to some of the most important developments in modern physics.

Maxwell studied at Edinburgh University and later at Cambridge. In 1849, he began researching colour vision, including colour blindness. In 1861, using the first colour photograph (of a tartan), he proved that all colours can be made from the primary colours of red, green and blue. He also studied the rings of Saturn, showing that these are made up of many small bodies in orbit.

Maxwell went on to make the discovery for which he is most famous. It was already known that magnets and electrically charged objects are surrounded by 'fields', or areas of influence. Using experimental work he showed that the forces within these fields travel in electromagnetic waves, and that these move at the speed of light. This, he realised, was not a coincidence, and proved what Faraday had suggested, that light must be an electromagnetic wave, and related to electricity and magnetism.

In his later career, Maxwell and his wife Katherine – both devout Christians – studied the nature of gases. They developed the ideas of earlier scientists, that gases are made up of constantly moving molecules. They discovered that this movement depends on the

The electromagnetic spectrum

The electromagnetic spectrum is the complete range of all electromagnetic waves. These waves travel through space, like ripples on a pond. They move at nearly 300,000 km a second, and vary in length. Radio waves, for example, can be up to a kilometre long. The shortest are radioactive gamma rays, which are around 0.01 billionth of a metre long. The light rays we can see are called the 'visible spectrum', and form only a tiny part of the complete spectrum.

James Clerk Maxwell's work on the electromagnetic spectrum had a huge influence on the scientists of the 20th century.

temperature of the gas, and that heat is stored in gas in the movement of its molecules.

In 1874, Maxwell became the first Cavendish Professor of Experimental Physics at Cambridge. He set up the world-famous Cavendish Laboratory – the University's department of physics.

Albert Einstein (1879-1955), perhaps the greatest physicist ever, said Maxwell's work was, '... the most profound and the most fruitful that physics has experienced since the time of Newton.'

27

ERNEST RUTHERFORD
SPLITTING THE ATOM

BORN Nelson,
New Zealand,
30 August 1871
DIED Cambridge,
19 October 1937
AGE 66

Ernest Rutherford is best known for his work on atoms and radioactivity, and is recognised as the scientist who started and developed the science of nuclear physics.

Rutherford in the Cavendish Laboratory, Cambridge, where he worked on atoms.

Rutherford attended the University of Wellington. In 1894, he travelled to England and took up a post as a research student at the Cavendish Laboratory in Cambridge.

In 1898, he became Professor of Physics at McGill University in Montreal, Canada. There, he and a British colleague, Frederick Soddy (1877-1956), discovered that radioactive substances give off two kinds of particles, which he called alpha, beta (beta particles are, in fact, electrons), and gamma rays. Rutherford and Soddy realised that radioactive elements gradually 'decay', losing some of the particles from which their atoms are made. This led Rutherford to understand more about how atoms are made, and that their structure can be altered.

Later, in 1911, when working in Manchester, he experimented with bombarding a thin film of gold with alpha particles. Most passed through the gold, but some bounced back. Rutherford said this was as if a naval shell had been fired at a piece of tissue paper – and bounced back. He realised that this suggested that most of each gold atom was empty space, through which the particles could pass easily, but that its mass must be concentrated in a tiny space. This was the immensely dense nucleus, at the centre of an atom.

From 1917, back at the Cavendish Laboratory, Rutherford discovered that it was possible to break up this nucleus, using alpha particles. This is often described as 'splitting the atom' – once thought impossible.

Rutherford received the Nobel Prize for Chemistry in 1908, and his colleague Frederick Soddy received it in 1921. Rutherford was knighted in 1914, and was created Baron Rutherford of Nelson in 1931. 🇬🇧

Working with atoms

There were several pioneers in the study of atoms. **JOHN DALTON** (1766-1844) was the first person to put forward the theory that all elements are made up of tiny particles called atoms, and that all the atoms in an element are the same as each other, but different from the atoms in other elements in terms of their mass. **SIR JOHN JOSEPH THOMSON** (1856-1940) discovered the electron, an achievement on which Rutherford was able to build his own work. **SIR JAMES CHADWICK** (1891-1974) was Rutherford's assistant in the 1920s. He and Rutherford worked together on bombarding atoms with alpha particles to make them disintegrate. In 1932, Chadwick discovered that the nucleus of an atom contains particles we call neutrons.

JOSEPH ROTBLAT
PHYSICIST AND PEACE CAMPAIGNER

BORN Warsaw, Poland,
4 November 1908
DIED London,
31 August 2005
AGE 96

Joseph Rotblat was a physicist and a campaigner for peace. His message to scientists was: 'Above all, remember your humanity.'

Rotblat's family was too poor for him to go to university, so he worked as an electrician, and studied for a physics degree in the evenings. In 1939, he left Poland for Liverpool University, to work with Sir James Chadwick (see page 29), hoping his wife could join him. When World War II broke out, she was trapped in Poland.

In 1944, fearing that the Germans were developing a nuclear weapon (an atomic bomb), and believing that the Allies should do the same, Rotblat joined the Manhattan Project – a team of scientists in the USA who were developing a nuclear weapon.

However, it became clear that the Germans were not making an atomic bomb, and that the Americans planned to use theirs to threaten the Russians. Rotblat felt that this, and the arms race he feared would follow, was wrong and dangerous. He returned to Britain just before the Americans dropped an atomic bomb on the Japanese city of Hiroshima.

Rotblat went to work at St Bartholomew's Hospital, London, researching the effects of radiation. After the war, discovering that his wife had died in Poland, he decided to stay in Britain, becoming a citizen in 1946.

He never married again. Instead, he threw himself into his work, and into campaigning for world peace and an end to nuclear weapons. In 1957 he

Using the atom bomb

In 1945, the US dropped two atom bombs on Japan – on the cities of Hiroshima and Nagasaki. It is thought that over 200,000 people – mostly civilians – died, and the two cities were completely destroyed. Rotblat, like many other people, believed that this should never happen again, and that the world should get rid of these terrible weapons.

helped found the Pugwash Conferences on Science and World Affairs (named after Pugwash, Canada, where it first met). This organisation brings together scholars from all over the world to look for peaceful solutions to world problems.

Rotblat and Pugwash were awarded the Nobel Peace Prize in 1995. He was knighted three years later. 🇬🇧

Joseph Rotblat, winner of the Nobel Prize for Peace in 1995.

DOROTHY HODGKIN
PIONEER IN X-RAY CRYSTALLOGRAPHY

BORN Cairo, Egypt,
12 May 1910
DIED Shipston-on-Sour,
Warwickshire,
29 July 1994
AGE 84

Dorothy Hodgkin was a pioneer in X-ray crystallography – the study of crystals using X-rays. This is important in finding the shape of molecules – which can affect how they behave and what they do.

Dorothy Hodgkin in her laboratory. This picture was taken in 1964, the year she won the Nobel Prize for Chemistry.

Dorothy Hodgkin was born Dorothy Crowfoot, in Egypt, where her father was an archaeologist. Her parents then moved to Sudan, where she spent her early childhood. She attended a boarding school in England at a time when it was so unusual for girls to be interested in science that she had to travel to a nearby boys' school to study chemistry.

Dorothy went on to study chemistry at Oxford University, before moving to Cambridge to become assistant to another X-ray crystallography pioneer, John Desmond Bernal (1901-1971). In 1934, she returned to Oxford, working there until her retirement in 1977. She married in 1937, changing her name to Dorothy Hodgkin.

She always believed her most important work was in the study of insulin. This substance, which is enormously important to the human body, is extremely complicated, and it took her over 30 years to complete her work on it. Throughout her career, she travelled extensively, advising laboratories and giving talks on the importance of insulin in relation to the condition diabetes.

She also studied the structure of penicillin and the vitamin B12, making it possible for science to find ways of creating synthetic chemicals to treat a range of diseases. From 1960 she was a Research Professor at the Royal Society.

Dorothy Hodgkin was a socialist and a campaigner for world peace. She was president of the Pugwash Conferences (see page 31) from 1976 to 1988. When she won the Nobel Prize for Chemistry in 1964, she was only the fourth woman ever to win the prize in science.

The Braggs and X-ray crystallography

SIR WILLIAM HENRY BRAGG (1862-1942) and his son, SIR WILLIAM LAWRENCE BRAGG (1890-1971), together founded the science of X-ray crystallography. In 1915, the Braggs shared the Nobel Prize for Physics: the only father and son team ever to do so. William Lawrence, at the age of 25, was the youngest-ever prizewinner.

William Henry Bragg studied at Cambridge University and then took up posts at Adelaide, Leeds and London universities. During World War II he worked on submarine detection. His son, William Lawrence, also studied at Cambridge and took jobs at Cambridge and Manchester universities.

The Braggs investigated radioactivity and studied X-rays in particular. Together they were able to see how X-rays were refracted by crystals. This gave clues to their structure and was the beginning of the study of X-ray crystallography.

ALAN TURING
THE FATHER OF MODERN COMPUTER SCIENCE

BORN London,
   23 June 1912
DIED Wilmslow,
   Cheshire, 7 June 1954
AGE 41

Alan Turing is often called 'the father of modern computer science', developing for the first time the basic theory of programming. He is also famous as a code-breaker in World War II.

As a child, Turing was a brilliant mathematician and went on to study the subject at Cambridge University. While he was at Cambridge he first began to understand how it might be possible to produce machines that could be programmed to solve any kind of mathematical problem. His ideas were among the first serious plans for computer programmes.

In 1937, he went to Princeton University in the USA, returning to Britain in 1939. When World War II broke out he went to work for the British government in the code-breaking establishment at Bletchley Park. Here, with colleagues, he developed a machine called the Bombe, which was able to break the secret Enigma codes the Germans were using to communicate with their armed forces.

Towards the end of the war he returned to work on computing and, after a short spell in first London and then Cambridge, he took up a post at Manchester University. In the late 1940s, while at Manchester, he developed the software for the first true computers, and wrote extensively about artificial intelligence. He drew up what is known as the 'Turing Test' – that a computer deserves to be called intelligent if it can

The Bombe

Alan Turing's Bombe was a vital piece of equipment in the war against Germany. The Germans used a machine called Enigma to send coded messages. This was a complex machine consisting of a keyboard and a series of wheels, each with the 26 letters of the alphabet on them. When a message was typed using the machine, it produced a coded message which, in theory, could only be decoded using another Enigma machine. The success of the Bombe in decoding these messages was vital to the war effort.

deceive a human being into believing that it, too, is human.

Turing's life came to a sad end. He had known he was homosexual since he was a boy. However, homosexual acts were illegal at the time, and Turing was arrested. The scandal that followed meant that he was disgraced, and forbidden to work on any government projects. He died of cyanide poisoning in 1954. It is usually believed that he committed suicide.

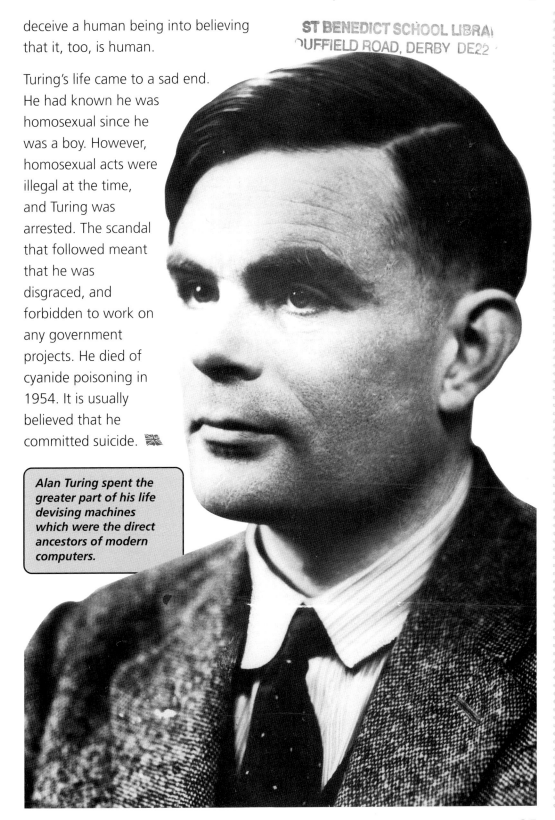

Alan Turing spent the greater part of his life devising machines which were the direct ancestors of modern computers.

FRANCIS CRICK
DISCOVERED THE STRUCTURE OF DNA

BORN Northampton,
8 June 1916
DIED San Diego,
California,
28 July 2004
AGE 88

With his American colleague James Watson and New Zealander Maurice Wilkins, Francis Crick made one of the most important discoveries of all time: the nature of the material that is responsible for genetic inheritance.

Rosalind Franklin

Crick and Watson's discoveries might have been impossible without the work of **ROSALIND FRANKLIN** (1920-1958).

Rosalind Franklin attended Cambridge University and worked in France before taking up a post at King's College, London. There, she worked on X-ray crystallography (see page 33) with Maurice Wilkins. When Franklin took an X-ray photograph of DNA that suggested that its form was that of a double helix, it was Wilkins who passed this on to Crick and Watson.

Rosalind Franklin had a stormy working relationship with Maurice Wilkins and felt that she had been sidelined over the issue of DNA. She eventually left King's College to take up a job at Birkbeck College, where she did important work on viruses until her early death.

By the 1940s, scientists had come to understand that the information about how a living thing develops is stored in the nucleus of its cells and is passed on from parent to offspring, and from cell to cell as the organism grows. They knew that a substance called deoxyribonucleic acid (DNA) made this possible. Finding out how the molecules of DNA were structured was vital to understanding how it works.

Crick studied at University College, London, and met James Watson (born 1928) while both men were working at the Cavendish Laboratory, Cambridge. The two shared an interest in DNA. Together, they studied information that other scientists had gathered. This included photographs Maurice Wilkins (1916-2004) and Rosalind Franklin (see left) had obtained at King's College, London, using X-ray crystallography. They worked out the structure of the DNA molecule – a 'double helix', like a

The double helix

DNA is a molecule that carries the information it needs to work in long chains, in the form of a 'double helix' – two long chains forming a kind of twisted ladder, with pairs of chemicals, called bases, acting as the rungs. The order in which these bases occur is a 'code' that carries the genetic information stored in every cell of a living thing. The two chains are mirror images of each other.

The cells of living things are constantly splitting in two, in order to grow, or to replace cells that have died. As a cell splits, each part gets one-half of the double helix – which can be copied, to make a new double helix, carrying the same information as its 'parent'. (There is more about DNA on page 41.)

Francis Crick with a model of the DNA double helix.

twisted ladder with 'rungs' linking the two parts. This structure makes it possible for DNA to carry an incredibly complex coded sequence of information, often described as the 'key' to life.

Crick, Watson and Wilkins won the Nobel Prize for Medicine in 1962. Sadly, Rosalind Franklin's early death meant she could not share this honour. 🏴󠁧󠁢󠁥󠁮󠁧󠁿

STEPHEN HAWKING
THEORETICAL PHYSICIST

BORN Oxford,
8 January 1942

As a child, Stephen Hawking was interested in astronomy. It is for his work in this field that he has become most famous, and for his book *A Brief History of Time*.

Hawking studied physics at Oxford University before going on to further studies in cosmology at Cambridge University. He continues to work at Cambridge University.

Hawking is probably one of the world's most famous physicists – but not only for his ground-breaking theories about space and time. He is also known as a long-term survivor of an extremely debilitating condition, amyotrophic lateral sclerosis (ALS). When he fell ill, at the age of 21, doctors said he was unlikely to live for more than five years. Yet he has managed to survive for more than 40 years. Although paralysed and able to speak only by using a computer and a voice synthesiser, he still manages to work, travel, lecture and write.

The area of theoretical physics in which Hawking works is extremely complex, and is concerned with the origins of the universe. His best-known work concerns black holes, which are generally believed to be collapsed stars. These are so dense that, although they appear small, they emit gravity so powerful that nothing, even light, can escape them. However, they are surrounded by a 'halo' of radiation.

This study led Stephen Hawking to form complex ideas about the nature of the universe, how it began and how it is developing. He suggested that the universe can be finite, but at the same time have no boundaries. He has tried to form what people have called a 'grand unified theory' about how the universe works – taking into account ideas put forward by great scientists of the past, including Sir Isaac Newton (see pages 10-11) and the German-American genius, Albert Einstein.

In 1988, he published a book outlining his ideas, *A Brief History of Time*. Millions of copies were sold, but it is often said that few people have understood it.

Stephen Hawking is remarkable in that he continues to work, despite being almost unable to move.

SIR JOHN SULSTON
MAPPING THE HUMAN GENOME

BORN Buckinghamshire,
24 March 1942

Sir John Sulston is a leading figure in the Human Genome Project. Completed in 2003, this project identified all the genes that make up a human being.

Sulston studied at Cambridge University, where he specialised in organic chemistry – the study of the substances that make up living things.

After working in the USA, he returned to Cambridge, where his research concentrated on a particular kind of worm. He recorded the sequence of the bases (the pairs of chemicals

Sir John Sulston's work on genomes has, he believes, provided 'a new and firm foundation for biological research'.

Genes and the human genome project

Genes are the units of hereditary material that are contained in the cells of living things. They are segments of DNA. The genes carry information about how the living thing will develop.

The complete map of genes is called the genome, and it can be found in the chromosomes of living things. A chromosome is a strand of DNA, with a coating of protein. The importance of mapping the human genome is that it may help in medicine, helping to develop new tests for diseases, new treatments and to create new drugs.

The Human Genome Project was undertaken by scientists from all over the world, mostly in the USA and by Sir John Sulston's team in the UK.

that join the strands of DNA – see box page 37) along the strands of the worm's DNA and where genes for particular qualities appear on the DNA molecule. This is called 'mapping and sequencing' the worm's genome.

Sulston then became head of the Sanger Centre, near Cambridge. The Centre, now called the Wellcome Trust Sanger Institute, is taking part in the worldwide study of the human genome. Sulston led a team of several hundred scientists who were mapping and sequencing one third of the human genome. The project was more difficult than his study of worms, because humans are much more complex organisms. The group also studied the genomes of other living things,

such as the bacteria that cause serious diseases, including tuberculosis and leprosy.

Sulston is particularly well known for his belief about how scientists should work together. Many privately-owned research organisations want to restrict their discoveries about the human genome, so that other scientists cannot use them, and so that they themselves can use the information they have discovered for profit. He has said that he considers this 'totally immoral'. Instead, he believes passionately that: 'From sharing, discovery is accelerated in the community. Research is hastened when people share results freely.'

John Sulston received a knighthood in 2001. In 2002, with US-based Sydney Brenner (born 1927, in South Africa) and Robert Horvitz (born 1947 in the US) he won the Nobel Prize for Physiology. 🏴󠁧󠁢󠁥󠁮󠁧󠁿

JOCELYN BELL BURNELL
DISCOVERED PULSARS

BORN Armagh, Northern Ireland, 15 July 1943

Jocelyn Bell Burnell made her most important discovery – the first pulsar – while she was still a graduate student at Cambridge University.

As a child, (Susan) Jocelyn Bell lived close to the Armagh Observatory. Staff there encouraged her interest in astronomy, but her plans were almost ruined when she failed her 11-plus examination – and so could not go to an academically challenging grammar school. However, her parents managed to send her to a boarding school, after which she went to Glasgow University.

Moving on to Cambridge, she studied for her PhD with Professor Antony Hewish (born 1924). There, in 1967, she made the discovery for which she is most famous. She had spent two years helping with the construction of a radio telescope. While using this, she detected a signal so regular that it could almost have been a sign of distant, intelligent life. This was so strange that she jokingly called it 'LGM' ('little green men'). However, astronomers soon realised that the signals were coming from a rapidly rotating neutron star, which we now call a 'pulsar'.

In 1974, Hewish and his colleague Martin Ryle (1918-1984) were awarded a Nobel Prize for Physics. Bell (by now using her married name, Burnell) was excluded, as she had only been a graduate student at the time of the discovery.

Since the discovery, Burnell has continued to teach, often travelling abroad to undertake research and give lectures. She was Professor of Physics at the Open University and then Dean of Science at the University of Bath, until she retired.

Why do pulsars pulse?

Pulsars are a kind of neutron star – stars that have 'died' and collapsed, so that they are small, but extremely dense. Some neutron stars rotate rapidly, giving off beams of energy from their poles. Because they are rotating, these beams can only be detected at regular intervals – and so they appear to be pulsating. Put simply, pulsars are the remains of a star after it has exploded.

Jocelyn Bell Burnell has said: 'One of the lovely things about working in astronomy is the number of surprising things that just keep rolling in.' Pulsars were just one of those surprising things. 🏴

Jocelyn Bell Burnell made her most important discovery – the existence of pulsars – while she was only 24, and still a student.

SUSAN GREENFIELD
EXPLAINING SCIENCE TO PEOPLE

BORN London,
1 October 1951

Susan Greenfield leads important research into the human brain, and how damaging conditions within it can be treated. She is talented at explaining science to people.

Susan Greenfield is a neuroscientist (a scientist whose area of study is the brain) who studied first at Oxford University, followed by spells in both New York and Paris. She is now Professor of Pharmacology (the study of drugs and their effects) at Oxford University.

Her main area of research is into the causes and treatments of two incurable conditions which affect the brains of many people, especially as they grow older. These are Parkinson's and Alzheimer's diseases (see box).

She is also interested in the way the human mind works, and what we mean by consciousness. When we think, the neurons (nerve cells) in our brains form temporary links, which are triggered by things in the outside world, or by thoughts, and which come and go, as she says, 'like clouds in the brain'. She has researched into how this happens, and has also considered how brain activity develops in babies and children.

In recent years, she has studied the way technology can affect the way the human brain works.

Alzheimer's and Parkinson's diseases

Alzheimer's disease affects up to a third of people over the age of 80. It is caused by the nerve cells in the brain gradually ceasing to work properly. Alzheimer's develops slowly, starting with simple forgetfulness, and ending up with the person affected being completely unable to look after themselves. It is incurable.

Parkinson's disease is caused by the slow destruction of the nerve cells within the part of the brain that controls movement. It begins with slight shaking, and ends with the person being almost unable to move. It is not possible to stop the cells from dying, but there are drugs that help control the symptoms.

Susan Greenfield has always worked hard to bring an understanding of science – especially her own area of study, the brain – to the general public. This has involved writing several books, which include: *Journeys to the Centres of the Mind* (1999) and *The Private Life of the Brain* (published in 2000).

She also appears on radio and television and gives public lectures. In 1994, she was the first woman to give the Christmas lectures at the Royal Institution.

Susan Greenfield has received a number of awards and, in 2001 she was made a life peer, Baroness Greenfield, which means she can sit in the House of Lords.

Susan Greenfield is a scientist, writer and member of the House of Lords. She has a talent for explaining science to the non-scientific public.

Glossary

acceleration The rate of change in the speed of a moving body.

alchemy An ancient science, the ancestor of chemistry. Alchemists studied a range of substances. One of their aims was to change less valuable metals into silver or gold.

artificial intelligence The ability of a computer to think and work like a human.

astrologer Someone who studies the positions and movements of the stars and planets, believing that they have an effect on world events and people's lives.

astronomy The science of all the bodies in the universe – the Sun, the planets and all the stars.

atomic bomb (atom bomb or nuclear weapon) A very powerful weapon that works by changing the nuclei of atoms – a process that releases huge amounts of energy.

atom The smallest part of an element.

bacteria (singular, bacterium) Tiny living things, too small to be seen without a microscope.

cell The smallest part of a living thing.

chromosomes Thread-like structures in the nuclei of the cells of living things. They are made up of a long molecule of DNA, with a coating of protein.

comet A small body made up of a ball of rock, dust and ice that orbits the Sun.

compound A substance in which the atoms of two or more elements are combined together.

compressed Pressed together to make smaller in volume.

DNA (deoxyribonucleic acid) The substance which carries information nearly all living things need to make them what they are – that is, their genes.

dynamo A machine that changes some other form of power directly into electricity.

electric generator A machine for making electricity.

electric charge The property some objects have that causes them to exert forces on each other.

electromagnetic force One of the four fundamental forces in nature, that hold everything together. The others are gravity, the weak nuclear force and the strong nuclear force.

electromagnetic induction The use of a magnet to produce electricity.

electromagnetic radiation Waves of energy that can travel through space and matter. They range from very long radio waves to very short gamma rays.

electromagnetic waves Oscillating (moving to and fro)

magnetic fields travelling through space.

electron A negatively-charged particle with almost no mass, that forms the outer part of an atom.

element A substance that cannot be split up into simpler substances.

energy Something that causes an action. Whenever anything happens, one kind of energy is changed to another.

evolution A gradual change, over many generations of living things.

fossil The cast or impression, or the actual remains of a living thing, preserved in rock.

gas Matter in a form that has no fixed shape or volume.

gene The units of the material that controls heredity – a section of DNA carrying certain information.

genetic To do with genes.

gravity The natural force which causes objects to be drawn towards each other, especially towards the Earth.

human genome The map of the position of, and the function of, all the genes on a human chromosome, together with the differences in individual genes that are responsible for variations.

magnetic field The area around a magnet where its force can be detected.

magnetism An invisible force around a magnet or an electric current, which attracts iron or other magnets.

molecule The smallest part of an element or compound that can exist independently.

neuron Also known as a nerve cell – a cell that transmits messages from one part of the body to another.

neutron An uncharged particle in the nucleus of an atom.

nucleus The central part of an atom or a cell.

palaeontology The study of fossils.

prism A triangular block of transparent material, such as glass, used to 'bend' a beam of light, or to split it up into the colours that make up the beam.

proton A positively charged particle in the nucleus of an atom.

radio telescope An instrument used to detect radio waves that are sent out by objects in space.

radioactivity The emission of high-energy rays from some elements.

spectrum The whole range of electromagnetic waves, separated into their constituent parts, ranging from long radio waves to short gamma rays.

thermodynamics The branch of physics to do with the transformation of heat into other forms of energy.

X-ray A form of electromagnetic radiation.

Some useful websites

http://www.spartacus.schoolnet.co.uk/engineers.htm
Biographies of scientists and engineers from all over the world.

http://www.makingthemodernworld.org.uk/about/
Stories of discovery and invention from the 1750s to the present day.

http://nobelprize.org/nobel_prizes/lists/all/
The life stories of all Nobel prize-winners in all fields – including science.

Note to parents and teachers:
Every effort has been made by the Publishers to ensure that the websites in this book are suitable for children, that they are of the highest educational value, and that they contain no inappropriate or offensive material. However, because of the nature of the Internet, it is impossible to guarantee that the contents of these sites will not be altered. We strongly advise that Internet access is supervised by a responsible adult.

SOME PLACES TO VISIT

Woolsthorpe Manor, Lincolnshire
The birthplace of Sir Isaac Newton, with hands-on science equipment.

Science Museum and Natural History Museum, London
The Science Museum includes the history of just about everything to do with science. The Natural History Museum is in the nearby Cromwell Road.

Down House, Downe, Kent
Visit the house where Charles Darwin developed many of his theories.

The Museum of Science and Industry, Manchester
This offers opportunities to find out more about science.

The Mansion, Bletchley Park, Milton Keynes
Turing's Bombe has been rebuilt and can be seen here. There is also a computer museum.

The Philpot Museum, Lyme Regis, Dorset
This small museum has an exhibition of fossils.

Techniquest, Wales
Four science centres in Wales that specialise in science for children.

Satrosphere, Aberdeen
A hands-on science centre, with lots of activities for young people.

Index

These are the lists of contents for each title in *Great Britons*:

LEADERS
Boudica • Alfred the Great • Richard I • Edward I • Robert Bruce
Owain Glyndwr • Henry V • Henry VIII • Elizabeth I
Oliver Cromwell • The Duke of Marlborough • Robert Walpole
Horatio Nelson • Queen Victoria • Benjamin Disraeli
William Gladstone • David Lloyd George • Winston Churchill
Clement Attlee • Margaret Thatcher

CAMPAIGNERS FOR CHANGE
John Wycliffe • John Lilburne • Thomas Paine • Mary Wollstonecraft
William Wilberforce • Elizabeth Fry • William Lovett
Edwin Chadwick • Lord Shaftesbury • Florence Nightingale
Josephine Butler • Annie Besant • James Keir Hardie • Emmeline Pankhurst
Eleanor Rathbone • Ellen Wilkinson • Lord David Pitt • Bruce Kent
Jonathon Porritt • Shami Chakrabati

NOVELISTS
Aphra Behn • Jonathan Swift • Henry Fielding • Jane Austen
Charles Dickens • The Brontë Sisters • George Eliot • Lewis Carroll
Thomas Hardy • Robert Louis Stevenson • Arthur Conan Doyle
Virginia Woolf • D H Lawrence • J R R Tolkien • George Orwell
Graham Greene • William Golding • Ian McEwan • J K Rowling
Caryl Phillips • Andrea Levy • Zadie Smith
Monica Ali • Salman Rushdie

ARTISTS
Nicholas Hilliard • James Thornhill • William Hogarth
Joshua Reynolds • George Stubbs • William Blake • J M W Turner
John Constable • David Wilkie • Dante Gabriel Rossetti
Walter Sickert • Gwen John • Wyndham Lewis • Vanessa Bell
Henry Moore • Barbara Hepworth • Francis Bacon • David Hockney
Anish Kapoor • Damien Hirst

ENGINEERS
Robert Hooke • Abraham Darby • James Watt • John MacAdam
Thomas Telford • George Cayley • George Stephenson • Robert Stephenson
Joseph Paxton • Isambard Kingdom Brunel • Henry Bessemer
Joseph Bazalgette • Joseph Whitworth • Charles Parsons • Henry Royce
Nigel Gresley • Lord Nuffield • Harry Ricardo • Frank Whittle • Norman Foster

SCIENTISTS
John Dee • Robert Boyle • Isaac Newton • Edmond Halley • William Herschel
Michael Faraday • Charles Babbage • Mary Anning • Charles Darwin
Lord Kelvin • James Clerk Maxwell • Ernest Rutherford • Joseph Rotblat
Dorothy Hodgkin • Alan Turing • Francis Crick • Stephen Hawking
John Sulston • Jocelyn Bell Burnell • Susan Greenfield

SPORTING HEROES
WG Grace • Arthur Wharton • Kitty Godfree • Roger Bannister
Stirling Moss • Jackie Stewart • Bobby Moore • George Best
Gareth Edwards • Barry Sheene • Ian Botham • Nick Faldo
Torville and Dean • Lennox Lewis • Daley Thompson • Steve Redgrave
Tanni Grey-Thompson • Kelly Holmes • David Beckham • Ellen McArthur

MUSICIANS
William Byrd • Henry Purcell • George Frideric Handel • Arthur Sullivan
Edward Elgar • Henry Wood • Ralph Vaughan Williams • Noel Coward
Michael Tippet • Benjamin Britten • Vera Lynn
John Dankworth and Cleo Laine • Jacqueline Du Pre
Eric Clapton • Andrew Lloyd Webber • Elvis Costello
Simon Rattle • The Beatles • Courtney Pine • Evelyn Glennie